Christmas Music *for Easy Classical Guitar*

Arrangements by Amy Hite

Introduction

This is a collection of twenty-four Christmas songs arranged for easy classical guitar. The songs are somewhat arranged in order of increasing difficulty. Most of the music is in first or second position, and a few pieces explore higher notes on the fretboard. The songs are harmonized with many open bass notes, which is easier for the fretting hand. The arrangements are festive and fun to play.

Joy to the World

Arranged by
Amy Hite

Lowell Mason
1792-1872

Gabriel's Message

Arranged by
Amy Hite

Sabine Baring Gould
1834-1924

O Come, O Come Emmanuel

Arranged by
Amy Hite

Anonymous

Up on the Housetop

Arranged by
Amy Hite

Benjamin Hanby
1833-1867

Deck the Halls

Arranged by
Amy Hite

Anonymous

We Three Kings

Arranged by
Amy Hite

John Hopkins
1820-1891

We Wish You a Merry Christmas

Arranged by
Amy Hite

Anonymous

Jolly Old St. Nicholas

Arranged by
Amy Hite

Anonymous

Jingle Bells

Arranged by
Amy Hite

James Pierpont
1822-1893

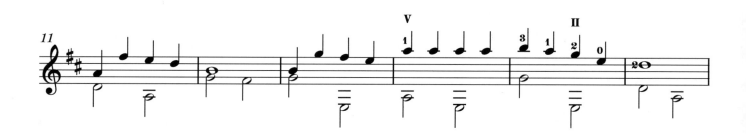

Auld Lang Syne

Arranged by
Amy Hite

Anonymous

I Saw Three Ships Come Sailing In

Arranged by
Amy Hite

Anonymous

The Holly and the Ivy

Arranged by
Amy Hite

Anonymous

Away in a Manger

Arranged by
Amy Hite

James R. Murray
1841-1905

13

Here We Come a Wassailing

Arranged by
Amy Hite

Anonymous

Hark, the Herald Angels Sing

Arranged by
Amy Hite

Felix Mendelssohn
1809-1847

Good King Wenceslas

Arranged by
Amy Hite

Anonymous

O Little Town of Bethlehem

Arranged by
Amy Hite

Lewis Redner
1831-1908

17

God Rest Ye Merry Gentlemen

Arranged by
Amy Hite

Anonymous

O Come, All Ye Faithful

Arranged by
Amy Hite

John Wade
1711-1786

Moderately

The First Noel

Arranged by
Amy Hite

Anonymous

O Christmas Tree

Arranged by Amy Hite

Anonymous

Angels We Have Heard on High

Arranged by Amy Hite

Anonymous

Silent Night

Arranged by
Amy Hite

Franz Gruber
1787-1863

Carol of the Bells

Arranged by
Amy Hite

Mykola Dmytrovych Leontovych
1877-1921

About the Author

Amy Hite is a music teacher living in Temecula, CA. Amy graduated Magna Cum Laude with a master's degree in Classical Guitar Performance from California State University, Fullerton. She held an Associate Professor of Music position at Riverside City College and served as the chair of the Guitar Syllabus Committe for the Certificate of Merit™ program with the Music Teacher's Association of California. She has an extensive performance background and has recorded three albums. She enjoys composing, arranging, and recording music. Amy is also a certified yoga and Alexander Technique teacher. More about Amy can be found at **www.AmyHiteMusic.com**.

Publications by Amy Hite:

Music Theory for Guitar: Levels 1, 2, and 3

Easy Christmas Music for Beginner Guitar

Christmas Music for Easy Classical Guitar

Folk Music for Easy Classical Guitar

Made in the USA
Las Vegas, NV
06 November 2024